A Golf Marshal's Chronicles

"What happens on the course stays on the course" until the Marshal tells all.

Author: Chuck Burgett, Ph.D.

Illustrations by: Don Felich

A Golf Marshal's Chronicles

Copyright © 2009 Chuck Burgett, Ph.D.

Illustrated by Don Felich

ISBN: 978-1-935125-68-6

Book printed in the United States of America

To order additional copies of this book go to:
www.rp–author.com/burgett

Robertson Publishing
59 N. Santa Cruz Avenue, Suite B
Los Gatos, California 95030 USA
(888) 354-5957 • www.RobertsonPublishing.com

CONTENTS

Introduction

In the beginning days of golf rules of play and conduct were carefully crafted and religiously adhered to by those fortunate to be playing the game. Golf, as most of you readers know, is one of the few, perhaps the only, sport that players themselves monitor the enforcement of the rules, call penalties on themselves and keep their scores. Golf has long been known as the gentlemen's game, a title well deserved. However, as time passed and more and more people got involved in the game some subtle and not so subtle changes occurred.

Once played almost exclusively on private golf courses by members only golf started to move to the realm of the common man and the development of the "municipal" golf course made it possible for everyone to play golf. With more and more players on the course, with a lower understanding of the traditional honor of the game, the game itself began to degrade. Most notably were a disregard for the physical golf course itself and most importantly the pace of play. Suddenly what used to be an enjoyable four-hour event in a beautiful outdoor environment became a six or seven-hour ordeal played on courses that resembled cow pastures or rugby fields. Something had to be done to restore the natural order and hence the exalted position of golf "marshal" was created.

The precise date and location of the first marshal has not accurately been recorded but they began to appear in the 1960's. The original charter was to patrol the golf course and assist golfers in following the rules of respect for the course and playing a faster round of golf. Obviously the best marshals were those that had good personal skills and those able to influence others. Unfortunately, not all marshals had or have those talents and consequently many conflicts between players and marshals occurred. It turns out that the perfect candidates for marshals come from the growing group of baby boomer retirees from management positions. These people wanted to play golf, interact with people and be outside and were willing to work basically for free but definitely for free golf.

I joined that group of gentlemen in the fall of 2000. The marshal job is a fun job and like all jobs it has its good points and not so good points. The golfers and their actions on the golf course provide one of the best points. The following pages will recount actual events that occurred on golf courses I have marshaled. Some names of the participants have been changed to protect the innocent but the stories are real. Although it may seem hard to believe these things did happen and just like they say in Las Vegas....

"What happens on the course, stays on the course", until the marshal tells all.

CHAPTER 1

Friday Night Fights

"Its good sportsmanship to not pick up lost golf balls while they are still rolling." —Mark Twain

Golf is the Royal and Ancient game and is supposed to be played by gentlemen. Apparently even gentlemen can get annoyed, or shall we say mad, when playing this game. Yes, it is frustrating and often there are financial wagers placed on the game. Not to mention that a poorly struck shot can really raise anger, to the point of breaking clubs, throwing clubs etc. (more on that later). It is actually rare that two or more players decide to take out their anger on another player but it happens.

Working the last shift as a marshal can be pretty boring, basically you are one of the few people left on the golf course and the ones left playing have started late and want to get finished. This means that the golfers have less respect for the course and try to get away with the small rule violations, like driving on the fairways when it is cart path only. Many are just in a hurry to get finished and a significant group of others are just ready for another beer and the next hole. This can create a pace of play situation where one group, say the group in front, wants to relax, imbibe and take their time and the group behind wants to play quickly. Late one Friday night in July I was the late shift marshal. I came around the course to find two foursomes very close together; in fact a couple of the players were actually touching each other. Well, let me say that another way. They were fighting.

This was an amazing event to see. In fact it looked like a hockey game. Player one, we will call him Bob, had managed to get a good hold on player two, we will call him Frank. Bob had pulled Frank's golf shirt over Frank's head, tearing it as he did so and was proceeding to apply a series of body and face punches to Frank. Frank was in a bad situation but was doing a good job of counter punching blindly in the direction of Bob. Usually one plays golf with friends and so the other members of these two groups were starting to get involved in the affair. Good sense and experience teaches that when two people are fighting the best thing to do is let them finish, which usually doesn't take long, and then go in and sort things out. This was the tactic I had decided to employ until I noticed one of the other players grabbing a club and heading toward the fight with the look of knocking someone in the head with the club. That would not be a good thing and I drove my marshal cart into the foray. I was successful at cutting off the club attacker and, as expected both Bob and Frank had enough of the fight by that time so I could go over and restore order.

Here's how it went. Marshal, "Gentlemen, seems like we are a little upset, what happened? Bob, " These guys hit into us off the last tee and didn't even yell fore." Frank, wiping some blood off his face, " That's right, they are playing way too slow and won't let us through, they may want to drink but we want to play golf, anyway we didn't hit anyone." Bob, "Yeah, you couldn't hit a barn door from five feet and we would have let you through!" Marshal, "Ok, what happened next?" Bob, " I went over and picked up his golf ball." Frank, "Yeah, and I came up and asked for the ball back and he wouldn't give it to me, he said he was going to keep it." Bob, "That's when he went over to my golf bag, unzipped it and started taking my golf balls out of the bag. That's stealing and I grabbed him and pulled his shirt up and let him have it."

I had heard enough. "Ok, gentlemen. Golf is a gentlemen's game and does not include fighting. Now, please act like gentlemen, shake hands and think about playing as gentlemen the next time you come to the golf course. As for today, your round is finished and it is time to go back to the clubhouse and on home for the evening." Not totally happy both agreed and headed home.

CHAPTER 2
There are animals in the woods

"There's and old saying. If a man comes home with sand in his cuffs and cockleburs in his pants, don't ask him what he shot."
—Sam Snead

Golf courses are truly beautiful places. A splendid blend of water, sand, grass and trees. They are attractive to both man and animals. In some parts of the country even alligators are part of the golf course. Sorry, I don't have any alligator stories to share but I do have some animal stories.

In the springtime as the weather warms the cold-blooded animals begin to make an appearance. Where I work the cold-blooded animals are frogs, salamanders and most important snakes. There are many different snakes to be found on the golf course, garter snakes, king snakes, and gopher snakes and rattlesnakes. For some reason, even though all but the rattlesnakes are harmless to people, golfers seem to hate snakes. When they see a snake the most frequent response is to kill it, a truly unfortunate action for our reptilian friends.

However, when there is a snake situation on the golf course the marshal is most often called to solve it. Most of the requests are calls for a problem with a rattle-snake and most of the time, not always; the problem is really with a gopher snake. Gopher snakes do look a lot like rattlesnakes but they are usually much longer, up to four feet and they do not have a triangular shaped head or rattles. They are actually very useful for rodent control on the golf course. One fine June morning I was on the course when a call from the pro shop came to me to go to the fourth tee to remove two rattlesnakes from the tee box. When I got there I found not two rattlesnakes but two gopher snakes. They had selected the tee box for some rapid romantic activity and were not the least bit interested in the golfers or golf. The golfers were however interested in getting them off the tee box. To solve the problem I gently lifted them, as a pair, with a sand trap rake and moved them off the course providing them with privacy and allowing the game to go on. I don't think they even noticed that I moved them.

Gopher snakes also like to lay in the sand traps and warm themselves; to many golfers this creates a double hazard when their ball finds the trap. More than once I've had the opportunity to remove them safely from the hazard, always with a thank you to the golfer for not whacking the snake with a club.

There are, however, times when the snake actually is a rattlesnake. Most often they are in the deep natural grass, rocks and woods surrounding the golf course and we clearly mark these areas as do not enter rattlesnake habitat. Most golfers seem to lose the ability to read when their golf ball, worth less than five dollars, finds its way into these marked areas. These snakes do not want to bother you but when you step on them or their nest they will and do bite. The worst are the little "baby" rattlers as one of our golfers found out. He was lucky enough to not get bit by the snake when he found it next to his ball but he was stupid enough to grab it behind the neck and catch it to show his friends. His friends were impressed with the snake and one of them wanted to hold it too. During the attempted transfer the snake found its way to get enough room to bite the new holder and inject the full venom. By the time we got to him he was going into shock, fortunately we got him to the hospital and three anti-venom injections later he was stable. We liked to talk about it in terms of the ad for a popular credit card at the time. " Sleeve of golf balls fifteen dollars, round of golf $150, three anti-venom injections, $20,000, being able to read signs and follow directions, priceless."

The little rattlesnakes like to hide in places where it is cool in the afternoons. I was called to the fifth green on a nice June afternoon. Much to the surprise of one of our golfers he found his golf ball resting on top of one of these little rattlers in the cup. Fortunately he saw the snake before he reached for his ball and we were able to use a trash pick up tool to retrieve first the ball and then after the golfer had moved on, the snake.

You might expect snakes on the golf course but how about cattle? On a frost delayed October morning I got a call from the maintenance crew that there was a heard of cattle on the third fairway and could I please get them off the course. So off I went and sure enough there they were, all forty-three of them. They had entered the golf course; perhaps I thought through a hole in the fence and were now spread out in the rough, the sand traps, the environmental sensitive areas and the fairways. They were enjoying the new menu and did not want to leave. I decided to go after the largest bull that had gone the farthest on the course and see if I could get him turned and headed off the course. Of course the green was between the cattle and the fence and I had to ensure that they did not go across the green. I carefully approached him and got him started in the right direction, then the others began to run too, it was a funny scene as the grass was covered with frost and the cows were slipping and falling like bowling pins. Once I got them started I just chased them in the right direction, and they found their way quickly to an open gate and off the course. I closed the gate and the problem was solved. All in a days work for a marshal.

Wild pigs are another problem on the golf course. Usually they enter the golf course during the night and go foraging for acorns and grubs. They do a lot of damage to the golf course once they get on it so major efforts are made to keep them off by fencing. Still they find their way on but not always off. These animals, especially the boars, are not to be messed with, in fact they are down right danger-ous and aggressive, as one of our early am golfers found out. He was playing the third hole when he came across a large, actually very large, boar. He thought that he could just chase him away but the boar had a different idea and charged him. Luckily he found a nearby tree and climbed up just out of reach of the boar. Cell phones are generally not welcome on the golf course but in situations like this they can be very helpful, and he used his to call for help. Of course they send the marshal out to see what is going on. This time the only solution was to call for game management support. About and hour later a 350 lb boar was lifted from the course, to become some ones dinner and our golfer came out of the tree.

CHAPTER 3
Hit the Fairway not Me

*"A hundred years of experience has demonstrated that the game
is temporary insanity practiced in a pasture."*
—Dave Kindred - columnist

Practicing Marshals spend most of the day riding in their golf cart observing the play of golfers. The most effective way to do this is to ride the golf course in reverse order of holes, i.e. start at the eighteenth green and work your way back to the first. The reason for this is that it enables the Marshal to see where there are gaps, or open holes that indicate slow play and therefore address that problem in the most efficient way. The problem with riding this way is the golfers playing the hole are hitting their shots in the direction that the Marshal is coming from. Prudent marshaling therefore means to ensure that one keeps a practical distance and/or position out of the line of the next shot. Of course this means assuming the golfer will hit the ball where a) he should and b) where he is aiming. This of course does not always happen and when it doesn't you are endanger of being hit by the golf ball. The golf ball has hit my cart or me many times. Here are some of the most interesting.

Approaching the fourth tee box I noticed a foursome preparing to tee off. Fortunately the cart path I was riding on was wide to the left of the tee shot and I took a position about 200 yards from the tee box and stopped to watch the drives. Unexpectedly the first to hit hooked his shot right at my cart. I only had time to duck before the ball struck the plastic windshield.

Note: most golf carts have little warning signs that say that the windshield will not stop golf balls and this incident proved that fact. The ball hit the windshield and proceeded to smash right through it, striking the seat just right of me. The hole it left in the windshield looked like a smiley face and the people on the tee box certainly thought that it was funny but I of course did not. I threw the ball out into the rough and when the hitter came up he apologized, it was just luck that it didn't hit me.

Marshals are team players in an organization called outside services at most golf courses. Outside services provide customer services such as cart check in and out, club cleaning and loading clubs on carts and off, range services and range ball picking and starter roles on the first tee in addition to marshaling. Frequently, to provide variety to the day, the staff will rotate through these positions. This is how I got my opportunity to be the ball picker on the range.

The guy in the picker is often the target for the people hitting balls from the range. This is even encouraged by ads run for the PGA on television. "Let's see if we can hit the picker" is often a game for the range rats. This is not a fun game for the picker person. When the ball hits the picker it is a jolting noise at best. At worst, because the picker is not shot proof it is just dangerous. As a picker I have been hit many times while doing my job. Golf balls have come through the rear window of the picker, just missing me, one even landing in my cup of soda and others through the gaps in the cage around the doors, rattling around like pin balls inside the cockpit. One particularly obnoxious future outstanding golfer in the twilight of his career decided to hit me and was successful on three tries. That was enough. I just kept right on driving up on to the tee box and right at him. Luckily for him he grabbed his clubs and ran to his car. Give the picker guys a break and don't hit at them.

Marshals are not the only people that get hit on the golf course, other golfers do too. I was coming up the ninth fairway, which paralleled the first. I noticed a golfer on the ninth in the sand trap about 124 yards from the green. I also noticed golfers on the first tee. I stopped to wait for a break in the action. Just as the player in the sand trap started to hit his shot a player on the tee hit his. The tee shot was a duck hook and struck the player in the sand trap directly in a very sensitive area. The result was as expected, an immediate collapse in the sand with much pain. I went to the rescue and learned that it was his birthday and he was planning a big day. After the application of ice packs and a few moments of rest play resumed.

Not all incidents result in a happy ending. Coming over a hill I notice that a group of seven or eight players had convened in the third fairway, which paralleled the fourth. This does not normally happen so I went directly over to see what the situation was. One of the eight was on the ground and bleeding profusely from the back of his head. He had been struck by a tee shot and had a real bleeder. We immediately got emergency help out and applied pressure to the wound. Fortunately it was only a superficial cut but his day of golf was finished.

Golf balls are not the only objects that players get hit with. I was working as a starter on the first tee and a group of players were preparing to tee off. While they were talking and deciding on which game they were going to play one of the players was casually swinging his club. His buddy was not watching and as you can guess the club met the head of the buddy with a loud crack. Down and out for the count the foursome had now become a threesome.

CHAPTER 4

What do bears do in the forest?

"I'm hitting the woods just great, but I'm having a terrible time getting out of them" —Harry Toscano

It has been said that the entire world is a man's toilet and that certainly seems to be the case on the golf course. Countless numbers of "gentlemen" golfers find the urge to help the maintenance crew by "watering" any bush or convenient tree whenever the urge hits, much to the disgruntlement many other golfers especially the ladies. If you have ever played a round of golf you know that this is true. It surprises me that the men behave this way as golf courses in general have a layout that provides access to restroom facilities approximately every four holes. Given the current desired pace of play that should mean that once and hour a golfer will encounter a rest stop. I have discussed this issue with many head greens keepers and they assure me that they do not need any help watering the course so it would be appreciated if all golfers used the facilities.

In my experience I have found that men are not the only ones to take a pause for the cause on the course. The fifth hole is a wonderful par five. The tee is elevated with a well bunkered target area, the middle of the fairway is cut with a sharp drop off with very high rough and then the second shot, over this area is to a very well bunkered green. There is out of bounds on the right the entire hole and severe rough on the left. This is just a great hole. There is a very nice concrete structure behind the fifth green called a restroom. We had two lady golfers that were regular weekday golfers on the course. They were both pretty good golfers and seemed to be a happy couple. One was slightly built and the other quite portly. At the time the golf course was very busy and we usually only allowed foursomes on the course. Consequently the ladies were paired with two other golfers.

One magnificent California spring morning these ladies came to he course for the weekly round. They were paired with two young men and off they went. I was working my way around the course and came up behind the fifth tee. I couldn't believe my eyes. In front of me the larger of the two ladies was squatting behind the golf cart, shorts down to her knees, holding onto the bag rack and peeing like a race horse. This was not a pretty sight and I think it shall be indelibly etched in my mind forever. As soon as I came around the corner they saw me and up came the shorts. I drove up to them and went on by offering my good morning greeting, but I was wondering where the two young men were? I glanced down the fairway and saw them standing along the cart path waiting to go out and hit their second shots.

I drove up to them and they asked what had happened to the ladies. I related the story and all three of us had a good laugh. I told them that they were lucky that they had gone ahead and they agreed.

Accidents do happen in real life as well as on the golf course. On a crisp October afternoon I was making my rounds near the eight tee box, a short par three, guarded by woods on the right with a steep down hill grade in the woods to a small stream at the bottom. The woods are not maintained and contain all kinds of undergrowth, black berries and poison oak. We had an early rain and the slope was very soft and muddy. I noticed at the tee box there was a golf cart with a single bag but there was no golfer to be seen. This is an unusual event on a golf course so I stopped to look for the golfer. After a just and lawfully constituted search I was unable to find a golfer. I called out to see if anyone was around and a voice out of the woods answered back. I headed over to the edge of the drop off and yelled, "Are you all right?" The voice replied, "No, I'm not." I looked over the edge and there was a naked man, standing about twenty feet down the embankment. I asked, "What happened?" The man replied, "I was on my way to the tee box and I got diarrhea. I ran over to the woods and started down, then I slipped and started sliding down and everything came out, everywhere. My shirt, shorts, everything, is a mess, I need some help." Helping people is one of the best parts of the marshal job so I volunteered to help him out. I told him that if he would agree to go to the pro shop and pay for them I would go get him some new clothes. He happily agreed and I asked him for his sizes and off I went to the pro shop.

I related the story to the shop crew and after their laughter stopped I purchased a new pair of shorts, a shirt and a belt, grabbed a dry towel and a wet towel and went back to our distressed golfer. Man was he glad to see me. I threw down the towels first then the clothes and in a few minutes a well-dressed golfer reappeared from the woods. He was grateful and thanked me for the help. I think he thought his ordeal was over with but it wasn't because, did I mention that there was poison oak in the woods? I thought I had, and he was standing buck naked right in a big patch of it when I first saw him! Those of us working on the outside services provide a lot of services to the golfers and we appreciate tips once in a while. I personally have found and returned hundreds of golf clubs, cell phones, I-pods and even wallets and tips are almost never offered. Now this was a situation that should have generated a tip, but didn't. I think in retrospect I should have done something like this. "I'm back, I brought you a wet towel, a dry towel, new shorts and a shirt and a belt." Golfer, "Great thanks, let me have them." Me, standing, looking down and holding the goods, while silently waiting to hear more. Golfer, getting the idea, "Oh, yeah, " I have two dollars for you." Me, "Thanks, here's the belt." Golfer, " Oh, I meant five dollars." Me, "That's very kind of you sir, here is the belt and the dry towel." Golfer, "Did I say five? I meant to say twenty." Me, "Thank you very much, here is the wet towel, the dry towel and as soon as you are ready I'll give you the rest of the stuff."

CHAPTER 5
What's that smell?

"They call it golf because all of the other four letter words were taken." —Raymond Floyd

There is something extremely invigorating about spending a few hours on the golf course. The beauty of the course and the smell of green grass and flowers is enough to make most people euphoric. Nature itself however is not enough for everyone and "green grass" is not the only grass that can be smelled on the golf course.

It amazes me that some golfers try to play while using drugs, mostly marijuana, but they do. For several years we had a regular twosome that would come out late in the afternoon and hit the links. They were a very happy couple of guys and always friendly and nice to all of us at the course. They seemed to really enjoy their round of golf and part of their enjoyment was the sharing of a pipe with good grade grass. I guess they didn't think that others could smell the characteristic odor, or if they did it didn't bother them. More than once they would return from their round and check in their cart leaving some samples and the pipe behind in the cart. When the cart crew went to clean it they would find the pipe and we even made a special place to keep it.

When they returned for their next round the pipe would be returned to the owners with no questions asked and sly smiles around. Surprisingly, even playing in their high state they never caused a problem or had an accident with the cart while on the course.

While these regulars were pretty predictable in their activity they were by no means the only golfers to try to reach an elevated state on the course. Nor were they the only ones to leave evidence in the golf cart. I often think that the late night cart clean up crew kept their selves well supplied with just leftover bags of grass and joints in the golf carts.

Of course drugs are not the only mental state changers used by golfers. The most frequent is alcohol. The golf course owners encourage the drinking of beverages, even supplying traveling cart service to sell your beverage of choice directly on the course. I am positive that many of the craziest things I have seen golfers do can be directly related to the amount of alcohol consumed during the round. It is particularly bad when there are large corporate sponsored tournaments. These events come complete with hole in one contests for new cars, cheerleaders from the local favorite professional sporting team and the margarita hole, the tequila shots hole, the beer keg hole and any other number of ways to provide alcohol to the players.

The results are frequently amusing. Golfers will walk to the tee box and start their back swing and then fall down. They will bend over to pick up their ball from the cup and fall on the green. And, my favorite of all, is trying to get their ball out of the lake and falling face first into the lake. I guess they are having fun, at any rate they provide us with good laughs.

Problems do come with golfers that are high on something; most notably they have trouble navigating the golf cart they are riding in. When this becomes the case we have to remove them from the course.

The golfers are not the only ones that over indulge at these events. Frequently the volunteers at the alcohol holes over do their share of the liquids. Volunteers do have it rough on the course. They have to sit in the hot sun, if lucky covered by a tent, and be nice to the golfers for six hours.

I can understand them getting in the party mood and getting thirsty. One such event involved some attractive young ladies pouring shots and selling raffle tickets. When I escorted them out to the course there were five of them. During the course of the round I passed by and talked with them a few times and noticed that they were getting a little (a lot?) wasted, but they were doing their job.

When I went to get them at the end of the event there were only four. I asked about the fifth and the others said they didn't know where she was, that she had just left a little while ago. After taking the four in I asked around and no one had seen the missing fifth. It was now getting a little dark so I went back out to the course looking for our MIA. Luckily for her I found her "resting" in the bushes near a little stream about 100 yards from the tee box. Except for being unconscious and pretty muddy from her nose dive into the stream there didn't seem to be anything wrong with her. I carried her back to my cart and delivered her to the rest of her friends. I hope she had a good time.

CHAPTER 6

Water Hazards

"If I had known it was going in the water I
wouldn't have hit it there." —Mike Reid

Modern day golf courses are truly beautiful places. The grass is well mowed, usually with two or three cuts, i.e. the fairway, rough and deep rough, and the putting surfaces are large, cut everyday and rolled frequently. To give contrast to the fields of green course architects place hazards, things like sand traps (bunkers), creeks and lakes. The creeks and lakes are called water hazards and seem to be filled with some special kind of water that attracts golf balls. These water hazards are usually placed at precisely the place a golfer wants to hit, they are close to the greens, along the sides of the fairways and often across the middle of the fairway at about the distance of the average good tee shot. While the water hazards are pretty to look at they are a real problem for golfers, as a shot into the water usually results in one or all of the following: 1) one stroke penalty, 2) lost ball 3) another opportunity to try to hit over the hazard and 4) an opportunity to do 1-3 above again.

There is something about the water hazard that mentally affects golfers, even the best. If you are reading this book you probably remember the famous hole in the movie "Tin Cup". A golfer can go the entire day hitting the ball 100 yards onto the green but put water between him and the green and the same 100 yards and he will forget how to hit the ball and in the hazard it will go. Some golfers will go to great lengths to try to get the ball out of the hazard and others will just give it up. As for me, I will never take a ball out of a water hazard. I feel that if it went in there once it will do it again, and if I take it out of the water, put it back in my golf bag, it will tell all the other balls in my bag about how much fun it is to go in the water and then they will go in when I try to use them. It just isn't worth it to me.

It was a beautiful September day, just before noon and I was making my rounds of the front nine when I noticed a foursome of younger men playing the short par three fourth. The hole was beautiful, a tee shot of about 163 yards to a two tiered green with a small creek, about ten yards wide, running across just in front of the green. The four players were gathered near the creek. I could see three balls at various positions on the green but obviously one of the players had found the creek on his tee shot. I decided to watch to see what would happen next. Our poor unfortunate player, we will call him Sam, dropped his ball near the creek and prepared to hit what was now going to be his third shot, across the creek to the green some twenty yards away. It didn't seem to be Sam's day as his next shot barely left the ground and went into the creek. Not in the best mood Sam got another ball out of his bag and prepared to hit his now fifth shot. The result was not much better and another dimpled sphere was swept away in the creek. Sam was not getting happier but as one must in the game of golf he found another ball in his bag and repeated the scene. This time as his ball was headed down stream he walked over to his bag, grabbed it and carried it to the creek. He stood for a moment looking at the creek and then yelled, "Here damn it, take it all" and proceeded to throw his entire bag, clubs and all into the creek. Much laughter came from his friend and then he realized he needed the bag, clubs etc and had to remove his shoes and socks (fortunately he was wearing shorts) and walk into the creek and get his equipment. This seemed like a good moment to join the group and I did, just as he was coming out of the water with his totally wet equipment. By now it wasn't clear how the tempers were in the group. I said, "Not your best shot but a good throw." After a moment everyone was laughing and I asked Sam, "Why did you go in the water?" and he replied, "My car keys were in the bag!"

Most people do not throw their entire bag into the water, after all golf clubs and the rest of the equipment are expensive. However, people do throw golf clubs into the water. I guess that they figure, if the arrow hit it in the water I will get rid of the arrow. Please pardon the hunting reference there.

Some golf clubs will partially float when they are in the water. One beautiful spring day I was checking the course and came around the seventeenth green. A wonderful risk reward par five with an almost island green. I happened to notice what looked like the grip end of a golf club floating in the lake pointing like a monolith to the gods in the sky. I stopped and sure enough it was a golf club, head down in the water, shaft up in the air floating in the lake. The suspect club was about thirty feet off shore in the lake, I decided that I should get it out of the lake and being a good old farm boy from a mid America state I went and got a rope, made a lasso and after a half dozen tries brought the club in, a very nice two-iron hybrid. No one claimed it after a month so I fit it into my collection.

All water hazards are clearly marked with red stakes, meaning lateral hazard, or yellow stakes for direct hazard. I want to emphasize clearly marked. The eighth hole is a beautiful par four. The lone tree on the course is on the left of the fairway and a very small stream is along the right. If the tee shot is hit too far left the ball might be lost on the high fescue grass on the hill and if hit too far left the tee shot will go into the stream. The stream in clearly marked with red stakes. The tee box is well elevated and it looks like a driving hole. Mid summer is hot in Northern California and often windy. It was not a busy day on the course and I was making my usual rounds. I decided to stop on the tee box and look around at the pace of play. A group had just hit off the tee and was headed down the fairway. I watched them go and noticed I decided to stop on the tee box and look around at the pace of play. A group had just hit off the tee and was headed down the fairway.

I watched them go and noticed that one of the golf carts was headed straight toward the stream on the right. As I watched I wondered, what are they doing, don't they see the markers? Amazing, as all these stories are, I guess they didn't, the cart kept on going and drove into the stream. Of course it was now very stuck. Time for the marshal to go down and see what is going on and off I went. When I got to the scene of the swamp the driver, we will call him Diver for this story, came over to me. We both looked at the golf cart, firmly in the water and he said, "What was I thinking?" I looked at Diver and he at me and we just smiled while I called in for a tractor to pull the cart out.

It is not possible to drive a golf cart across a lake unless there is a bridge to drive it on. This does seem obvious to most of us but not too all. The second hole is a challenging par three with the water hazard on the right of the green. One of the duties of a marshal is to go around the course before play begins and check to see if the pin placements are correct and also playable, and to look for situations left on the course from the night before that need to be corrected before play begins. Play slows down (in terms of number of players) in November and I was making my routine check going around number two. I happened to look over at the lake and I could see two unusual things. First, it looked like the top of a golf cart, in the lake and, second, it looked like a golf cart seat floating in the lake. I checked it out and both one and two were in fact exactly what was going on. One of the late tee times had driven their golf cart into the lake and the cart was definitely in the lake.

The seat had come off the cart, (they are on easy to remove hooks) and it was floating in the lake.

The mud in lakes on the golf course is like glue and it just sucks things into it. We managed to rope the seat and get it out but the cart was not going to move. The decision was made to drain the lake and then pull the cart out. Seemed like a good idea at the time but, as we drained the lake the cart moved farther into the lake. Now to plan B, we swam to the cart, hooked up a cable and pulled it out with a wench on a truck. A couple of lessons from this: 1) the seat cushion is a floatation device, should your golf cart ever land in the water (sounds like an airline announcement) and 2) when you get a golf cart at most places you sign as responsible, in this case it cost over $3K to the driver for damages to the cart and 3) do not drive into the lake with your cart.

Speaking of the mud. Trust me on this. It is not worth walking in the mud on the edge of a golf course lake to get yours, or anyone's golf ball. The odds are better that your shoes will get stuck in the mud and come off your feet than that you will get the ball. If you do get the ball and get out ok the mud is very difficult to get off, ok next to impossible. Oh, did I mention that golf balls talk to each other and you should never put a ball that went in the lake and came out, with a ball that is in your bag.

Now it is theoretically possible to hit the golf ball out of the water hazard but it is very difficult. Does anyone remember Mr. VanderVald in the British Open? Ok, so you want to hit it out of the water and save a stroke. First, here is how you do it. 1) Make sure that you can see at least half of the ball above the surface of the water. 2) Play it like a sand shot hitting behind the ball and follow through high. The water will get to the ball faster than sand does and there is no bounce help so the follow through is very important. 3) Be sure and call the marshal over to watch the shot, and also all of your friends, because you are going to get very wet and muddy and it will be a good laugh. We marshals like good laughs. If you are lucky you will not fall in the water, which of course makes you happy but diminishes the laughter from those of us watching you.

As mentioned earlier the way to cross the lakes and creeks is over a bridge, it is however important that you use the bridges that are for golf carts, not the walking bridges. I know that sounds like a logical thing to say, and who would ever try to drive across the foot bridge with the golf cart but, I have more than one story where I have been called out to the course to help golfers with their cart high centered on the foot bridge. There is nothing to do to help you except get enough people to lift the cart and carry it off the bridge. It is amazing though how everyone one that tries this trick says, "It looked big enough to me."

CHAPTER 7

Where there's smoke, there's fire.

*"Golf fairways should be made more narrow. Then everyone
would have to play from the rough, not just me."*
—Seve Ballesteros

While golf course fairways, primary rough and greens are usually watered and maintained in a beautiful pristine green conditions, the tall rough and environmental areas are left pretty much natural. In Northern California our golf courses frequently have hills bordering them covered with natural grass. In the winter these hills are lush and green but in the summer they dry out and become the golden brown that California is famous for. Golfers try not to hit their ball into this grassy area in the winter because it is impossible to find the ball. However, as the grass dries it is frequently possible to not only find the ball but to also hit the ball out of the grass. Golfers do not like to lose balls and do not like to take extra strokes so they will go after the ball and try to play it in the summer.

There is one problem with playing the ball from this area. The grass is very dry and easily and rapidly burns. Because of that most golf courses have a no smoking policy during the hot months. Frequently there are rocks on or near the surface of the ground. Obviously if a golf club hits even a small rock there will be some damage done to the club, but that is not the real problem. The real problem is the fact that today's technology of titanium golf clubs causes a spark when the clubs hit the rocks, even sand. If you ever want to see the sparks just go to the driving range very early in the morning or after sunset and hit a few balls, you will see the sparks fly. Any way the combination of dry dust, dry grass and a spark inevitably results in the starting of a fire.

Mid July was a slow time on the golf course. The temperature was over 100 degrees and a hot breeze was blowing. The first hole was designed in a canyon with natural grass covered hills on both sides of the fairway. Our starters were instructed to inform all golfers of the fire hazard and no smoking policy and to also remind them not to hit titanium surfaced clubs out of the tall grass. Some people just don't seem to listen. After snap hooking his tee shot into the dry grass area on the left side hill our golfer headed up the hill carrying his utility club. After locating his ball, some two hundred yards from the green he made a mighty swing, hitting ball, ground and a partially covered rock. Faster than you can say fire he was surrounded by flames. Fortunately he was able to run away but in minutes the entire hill was aflame. It is a strange site to see fire trucks on a golf course and fighting a fire on a hill but that is what it takes to get the rapidly spreading fires out. Once the flames are out the blackened hillside is covered with marshmallow like partially melted golf balls that were lost in the grass during the winter.

When the winter rains come these blackened hills become slick, actually very slippery. This does not stop the intrepid golfer from trying to walk up them to retrieve or hit their golf ball. This usually results and very humors fall and free slide down the hill. Mud ground into expensive golf clothing does not come out easily, particularly if there is red clay in the soil. It is also not very attractive as a decoration for the remainder of the round.

If it were only golfers sliding down the hill it would just be humorous but some golfers take it to a higher level. They try to drive their golf carts up these slippery slopes. In boating it is very dangerous to get your boat parallel to incoming waves and the same rule applies to golf carts on the side of the hill. Unfortunately gravity has a way of turning the golf cart as it starts to slide and suddenly it is sideways and rolling down the hill. The end result is at best a ruined golf cart, broken clubs and a big bill to replace both and at worst injury to the players. These facts did not stop a foursome from trying to race up the slope on a December day. I saw them accelerating down the cart path and headed toward the muddy hill and watched in amazement as they headed up the slope. It didn't take long for the first cart to turn and start rolling down the hill throwing golfers and equipment onto the mud, it slammed into the second cart which joined the tumble like two lovers rolling in the hay. The carts leading the way the golfers following along sliding in the mud all tumbling down the hill. By the time I got to the scene there was a pile of smashed golf carts and four, fortunately, only muddy and uninjured golfers lying in the mud. Their day was over and there total investment was to include new golf clubs, bags and two new golf carts for the course.

CHAPTER 8
That's a nice shirt

"The difference between golf and the government is that in golf you can't improve your lie."

— George Deukmejan, former California Governor

Municipal golf courses do not typically have dress codes, meaning you can go out and play golf in just about any thing you want to wear. They also do not have marshals. Quality public golf courses will have a dress code and they do have marshals to enforce that.

The dress code is pretty standard. Men must have a collared shirt with sleeves, although thanks to Tiger Woods, a collared shirt now includes mock turtlenecks, no jeans or blue denims and no tee shirts. The same applies to women except they may wear non-collared tops but not tank tops or swimming suits. Of course clothes that are worn out are not allowed either.

These clothing rules are enforced on the entire golf course. At check in the pro-shop is supposed to refuse the purchase of a round if the dress code is not met. Again at the podium where carts are issued the code is checked and even on the practice range the code is enforced. The next to last check is at the starter on the first tee. The last is of course the marshal on the course. Customers are offered options, they can put on the correct clothes, cover up the incorrect clothes with rain paints or a jacket or purchase new clothes, or if on the course or range they can either change or go home.

Of course players try to get around this situation. More than once I have been making the rounds to see players in inappropriate clothing on the course. When confronted there is always and excuse, like it is too hot for the rain pants or I didn't know. Those excuses have no effect and they either change or off the course they go.

I do however have one story to relate that is far out of the ordinary. It was a hot August afternoon and the course was full. I was making my rounds and one of our regular players called me over. He told me that a few weeks ago his girl friend had been refused a place on the practice range because of her apparel. He accepted that but he complained that the group a few holes behind them had a player playing in a ragged sleeveless shirt. His question to me was, "Why aren't the rules enforced equally for everyone?" Of course I assured him that they were and that I would check it out. I went to the offending foursome and sure enough one of the players was dressed in a black shirt but the sleeves appeared to have been torn off at the shoulder.

I was impressed by the muscularbuild of the offender but not by his shirt. I confronted him with the rules explaining that he could not play in the shirt and did he have another. He immediately became angry with me and said that he did but it was collarless and he had been told at check in that he could not wear it so he had put on this $220 silk shirt and gone on the course. The shirt was too hot so he decided that he would ruin the shirt and tear off the sleeves so that he would be more comfortable when he played. Furthermore, he was not going to change again. Naturally I explained that he would have to leave the course then. He became angry and threatening. Ok, I will be back I told him. I then went to the other members of his group, which turned out to be his family, father, grandfather and son and explained to them that he was going to have to leave if he didn't change. They seemed to understand. But he still refused to comply and again threatened me. I offered to take his credit card and go to the pro-shop and purchase him a new shirt. He refused. In marshaling you have to have a back up for situations like this and that back up is the head golf pro. To end the confrontation I left and went to obtain the assistance of the pro. He told me to go ahead and remove the golfer from the course and sent me back out. Fortunately by the time I got back mister muscle had decided to put on a windbreaker and comply.

CHAPTER 9
Riding in a convertible

"Golf and sex are about the only things you can enjoy without being good at it." —Jimmy Demaret

The game of golf provides one with the opportunity for wonderful exercise while walking the beautiful course. Mark Twain even remarked that golf was a good walk spoiled, which is probably an accurate summation for many of us. To walk the golf course helps one get in good physical shape but also requires some athleticism to begin with. Many aging golfers found that they still loved the game but they could no longer lug their clubs around the course. Hence the invention of motorized golf carts.

Today's golf carts are really nice. They have compartments for balls, drinks, food, sometimes GPS systems, and a place to put clubs, bags and miscellaneous items, like jackets. They are governed so that they can only go so fast and that includes down hill. This is a necessary safety precaution as some drivers have the idea that golf carts are 1) four wheel drive vehicles and/or 2) joy ride machines. Furthermore, golf carts are expensive and the driver is liable for the safe keep and appropriate use of the cart, if not he is liable for the cost of repair or replacement. The combination of the fun factor and ignorance of the liability factor can create some interesting situations on the course. Water hazards have been discussed earlier but they are not the only hazards course architects strategically place on the golf course. Sand traps, or bunkers, are also hazards that the golfer must deal with. Sand traps can be cavernous in depth and are most often filled with soft sand. Golf carts are not designed to ride through sand traps. Never the less I found a golf cart and it's driver stranded in the middle of the left hand fairway bunker on hole eleven . When I drove up to see if I could help and asked what happened I was told, " I thought I could make it through." My thought was that I now had a new definition of "dumb" for the dictionary.

The edges of sand traps are usually cut cleanly and sloped toward the sand in the trap. This fact didn't strike one of my golfers when he decided to drive his cart right up to the trap before getting out to hit his ball. The weight of the cart plus two golfers, equipment etc. was enough for the cart to collapse the side of the bunker throwing the golfers and their cart into the trap. Fortunately, they were not hurt but the cart was virtually totaled and many of their clubs were broken. Again, when I asked what happened I was told, " I didn't know the ground was so soft." I now had one more new definition for "dumb". This event was of course expensive for the driver, as he had to pay for the replacement cost of the cart.

I thought I could make it through !

While I am on the subject of golf carts and sand traps I should mention, that while they go at a reasonably rapid pace, they are not designed to ramp up hills and jump over things, like sand traps. This fact seemed to escape four of my golfers on a nice Friday afternoon when they raced down a hill toward a steep sand trap and attempted to do a stunt jump over the trap. Both golf carts were buried in the trap nose down, four golfers had mild concussions and other cuts and injuries resulting in their ending their round, a ride in an ambulance to the hospital and associated costs, plus the replacement cost of the two golf carts. When asked why they did it they said, " It looked like it would be fun."

Golf carts also are not designed to go over large bumps like curbs in parking lots. That fact did not deter a pair of golfers from trying to drive their cart out of the parking lot over the curb instead of around through the path. Needless to say they were high centered on the curb with the associated damage. Good way to start the round.

Like all vehicles golf carts have a certain height and width. This fact means there are places that are two narrow to drive on, like pedestrian bridges, and to low to drive under, like trees.

I made my way around the thirteenth on a chilly March morning and found two golfers standing by their golf cart, currently located in the trees to the right of the fairway. When I went over to see what had happened I learned that they tried to drive under a tree and the branch was too low, hence the cart was wedged under the tree. They had been working for a significant amount of time, holding up play, trying to get the cart out from this sandwich, without success. I solved the problem by letting the air out of the tires, thereby lowering the cart, but also rendering it unusable for the rest of the round. I sent them on their way walking and reminded them that they would have to pay for the damages to the cart.

CHAPTER 10

Water, water, everywhere and not a drop to drink.

"Golf is a game invented by God to punish guys that retire early." —Red Green

Even in the deserts of the world golf courses stand as a beautiful oasis of lush green fairways and putting surfaces. It is a complex and difficult job to maintain the beauty and playability of the courses but extremely talented men and women greens keepers do an outstanding job. One of their major tools is the use of irrigation systems to water the green areas. Sometimes things don't go as planned with these aquatic assistants.

After a perfect drive down the middle of a long par five a group of golfers were preparing to hit their second shots just as they came into my view. The first to hit was in the middle of his back swing when the automatic (?) sprinkler system turned on directly in front of him. The blast of water was awesome and struck him with full force. I am sure that part of what happened was caused by the total surprise of the event, but the next thing I saw was a golfer, now soaking wet, knocked off his feet onto the ground. Of course his friends thought this was very funny until the sprinklers came on next to them and they got a similar treatment.

Sometimes the sprinklers will come on in the fairway after balls have been hit but before the hitter gets to the ball. This can present an interesting situation. The rules of golf require that you play the ball where it lies. In this case it means that you have to go into the sprinkler spray to hit your shot. It is always amusing to watch golfers try and figure out how to do that. Particularly since the sprinklers are overlapping in their spray patters so that while one is going past another is approaching. More than one golfer has been adequately drenched attempting to a) hit his ball or b) get it out of the sprinkler spray. In the spirit of assisting you golfers, and also in the name of improved pace of play I offer this helpful hint on what to do if the sprinkler turns on near you ball, preventing you from easily making the shot. Of course this advice only applies to those of you that are riding in a golf cart. If you are walking I wish you the best. Ok, so here is the tip. Drive your golf cart directly at the sprinkler and park it so the sprinkler head is under the middle of the cart. The cart will shield you from the spray and you can hit your shot, get in the cart and go quickly down the fairway.

Of course golfers sometimes unknowingly will cause the problem. If the golf cart hits a sprinkler head that is not fully retracted it can break it off. This is an amazing sight. It reminds me of the movies of the old days in the oil fields when they struck a gusher. The water pressure is very high in these sprinkler systems. I happened to see an unlucky twosome in a cart hit one of these sprinkler heads and knock it off. The water erupted and knocked their golf cart over onto its side, spilling both golfers onto the ground and giving them a total shower!

The greens are also watered by sprinkler systems. These areas are not immune from sprinkler events either. I remember it very well, it was mother's day, 2001 and the course was full of golfers, many families out for a celebration day on the course. On the eleventh green I saw a foursome gathered close to the hole, finishing their putts. Suddenly the sprinkler system turned on and all four got a cleansing. Note: you may try to run, but you cannot evade a maverick sprinkler.

CHAPTER 11
It's a mad, mad world

"I'm very even tempered on the golf course.
I stay mad all the time." —Bob Murphy

The peaceful tranquility of the pastoral golf course setting should encourage a relaxed sporting event. However, it often doesn't. Golfers, of all skill levels get very frustrated at the nuances of the game. A missed putt here, a shanked shot there, a ball out of bounds or into the lake, can raise the temperature of the golfer to near or above the boiling point. I think that a large part of the problem is that golfers think they are better than they are and set unrealistic expectations for the level of play. They invariably cannot live up to this high standard and so anger rises. As the anger raises so does the foul language, which penetrates the wonderful silence of the golf course. This proclivity for expletive language, by the way, is one very good reason not to purchase a home on the edge of a golf course. After the language peaks physical violence, usually taken out on the offending golf club, raises it's ugly head. This of course does nothing to improve the game and rarely makes the golfer feel better and does frequently have financial consequences to the golfer. I remember a few years ago at the ATT Pebble Beach Pro-AM one amateur was having a bad day and was really getting mad. His pro came over to him and calmly said, "Your not good enough to get mad, so calm down." What good advice that is for all golfers.

Angry golfers provide those of us working as marshals with some real entertainment. I was watching a foursome play a challenging par three, a well bunkered hole with a severe back to front drop, situated on a step hill side with very thick and long native fescue grass on the slop behind the green. One of the players had hit hs shot into this steep slope and his ball was buried deep into the fescue. He carried his wedge and putter with him as he searched for his ball. After he found the ball he tried to hit it out of the grass on to the green. Each time he struck at the ball he failed to accomplish the shot and with each strike his anger grew. Finally he got the ball out of the grass and then to express his frustration he threw his wedge about twenty yards. While walking toward the green the anger was still there and he slammed his putter down at the ground. It snapped into two pieces. He was now left, playing only the fifth hole with thirteen more to go and no putter to use.

While golf clubs do seem to be well designed for throwing, and can be thrown considerable distances, and often are, they are not well designed for landing. Quite often the landing proves fatal for the club, either breaking it or bending it. Either way the golfer is without its services for the rest of the day. Sometimes things, like trees, get in the way of the thrown golf clubs. My experience has shown me that golf clubs are particularly well designed for grabbing branches high up in trees and clinging on for dear life. Having tossed the club into the tree our intrepid golfer is now faced with a problem, either get the club out of the tree or abandon it there. It is most rewarding to watch the attempts to retrieve the club. Golfers will try throwing things at the club to get it down. Often they will use another club, which invariably has the same tree grabbing skills as its mate already in the tree and results now in two clubs in the branches of the tree. The next item used is the nearest sand trap rake. Rakes are even better designed for nesting in trees and so the rake or rakes find their way into the limbs as well. Of course attempts are made to climb the tree to get the club or shake the branches almost always without success. I think there are two reasons for this. One, golf shoes are not well designed for tree climbing and, two, the golf club really doesn't want to come out of the safety of the tree only to be mistreated by the golfer again and I think it moves farther out onto the narrow branches so it can't be retrieved.

Many times these clubs are thrown in the trees in the summer and can go un-noticed in the leafy branches all summer long. However, when fall and winter comes, and the branches bare, the clubs can be seen. One November day while marshalling I looked up at a large oak tree near the third green, just behind a very difficult bunker. To my surprise I saw not only a golf club perched high in the branches but four of the sand trap rakes as well! It was a slow day on the course so using the appropriate tools and ladders we retrieved first the rakes and then the, now very rusted, wedge from the tree.

Slamming a golf club into the ground is not the best use of a golf club. They do not always bend or break when smashed but they also don't forget that you did it and they will wait and get even with you later. The most common way is for the head of the club, weakened by the pounding, to fly off the shaft during a golf shot. This can happen on the practice range or even on the golf course. I once saw a golfer hitting to an island par three when his club decided to get even. He hit the ball and the head of the iron came off on impact and followed the ball like a fighter jet in combat. In the end both the ball and the head landed in the lake.

It is not uncommon to see golfers just take the offending golf club and snap it in two over their knee. In this case the punishment to both the club and the golfer are immediate. Rarely does the player seem to achieve the satisfaction of breaking the club that he expected. On one occasion I observed this destruction of equipment and I asked the golfer why he had broken his club. His reply, "Why not, it was mine?"

Total destruction of the club is not always the end result of the anger. Some golfers just punish their clubs for the poor performance on the course. I was in the parking lot of the golf course one day and I noticed one of our golfers tying a rope to the back of his car. Interested in this unusual activity I went over to see if he needed help. He said no, he was just going to tie his putter to the rope and drag it home to teach it a lesson!

CHAPTER 12
Slow play, some tips on how to avoid it

"If the following foursome is pressing you, wave them through and then speed up." —Deane Beeman

Much of the time and effort spent by marshals relates to helping players play their round of golf in a more timely fashion, in other words, ensuring a quick pace of play. The current standard for the pace of play is an average of fifteen minutes per hole, including time to look for golf balls, get a drink or a sandwich on the course or between rounds and any other activity done while on the course. This means the round should be completed in four and one half hours. Golf, of course can be played much faster than that and should be, but since the advancement of televised professional golf matches, many players think they need to take as much time as they see the pro's do. This of course is not the case and doesn't help them, their enjoyment of the game, or the enjoyment of players behind them. I thought it might be a good idea to provide a few tips on how to play a faster game of golf for the reader so that the marshal will not bother you and you can have a better time.

First, how do you know that you are playing too slow? Well a strong hint is that the group behind you is waiting for your foursome to hit their shots on every hole or every shot. The pace of play is to always keep up with the group in front of you, not the group behind you. When you have the group behind you waiting you run the risk of their anger and them hitting balls into you to speed it up. Even though Bob Hope once said, "If you think its hard to meet people try picking up the wrong ball." letting the group hit at you is not the best plan. Another hint that you are playing to slow is when the marshal comes by and asks you a question like, " I noticed you were falling behind the group in front of you and I was worried that you might be in trouble, is there something I can do to help you." Or he or she might say, " I am sorry, we forgot the TV cameras today so you can putt out a lot faster." If these two kinds of comments don't get you moving you can be sure that the next ones won't be as nice. Something like this, "If you don't catch up to the group in front of you I will have to pick up your ball and move you into position." It will not help you to give answers back like, "There's no one behind us waiting." Or, "We have been waiting for the group in front of us all day, they just now started moving." Marshals have heard them all, so just play faster.

One of the biggest reasons for slow play is gambling. This starts on the first tee where strokes are negotiated and games are determined. Get off to a good start, arrange your games, and wagers before you get to the tee. The tee box is a place to play golf not negotiate a game. When each hole is finished do not stand on the green to count strokes or pay off bets. Get in the cart and go to the next tee, there you can write down your score while the others in your group are hitting. Establish a "gimme" range for putts, don't mark your two-inch put and then wait for the rest to putt out.

The second major cause of slow play is lost equipment. This most often is lost golf balls, or soon to be lost golf balls, hit in the deep grass or trees. A good rule to establish is, " I won't look for your ball so don't look for mine." When the ball is in the deep hazards, just count it as lost and play on. Even if you find it you won't likely be able to play a good shot and you will save a lot of time. If, however, you want to help someone look for their ball in the rough a good rule of thumb is to look ten to fifteen yards closer to where they hit it from then where they think the ball ended up. You will be amazed at how many of their balls you will find, and how quickly too. Golf balls are not the only lost items; usually it is a lost club. Many times I have seen golfers going back holes to try to find their lost club, do not do this. Notify the marshal of the lost club and he or she can go back looking for it. However, before looking for the club or getting the marshal, always check your fellow players golf bag to see if your club is in their bag. Over ninety percent of the time this is where I "find" the lost club.

To play fast, play what is called "ready golf". That means go to your ball and when you are ready, hit it. This is not tournament golf and there is no reason to wait for other golfers to hit, just grip it and hit it. Ready golf applies to putting too. When you are waiting for your turn to putt get your ball lined up, read the green and be ready to play, don't wait for your turn to start reading the green. Continuous putting also really helps. Hit your first putt and then if you need to putt again, do it, don't mark the ball and wait.

Finally, take advantage of the ESC, or equitable stroke control. The ESC was set by the USGA to allow for fair handicapping but it really helps the pace of play. The ESC is the maximum number of strokes you can post for a given hole. It is based on your current index and is used to adjust your score before posting. The ESC is available at every golf course near the posting area. The way it works is like this. If the ESC for your index says the maximum number of strokes you can have on a given hole is a double bogey then when you post your score the maximum you use would be a double bogey. Apply that to your play on the course. When you get to a double bogey, stop playing, put your ball in your pocket and move on. That will really help the pace of play. Of course you cannot do this in tournament play but we are talking pace of play for recreation.

Lastly, let faster players play through your group if there are open holes in front of you. This will make you friends with those behind and keep the marshal away.

Follow these suggestions and you will have an enjoyable, quick round of golf and the marshals will love you on their course.

LaVergne, TN USA
10 February 2010
172771LV00001B